$10.00

D0665431

Forgiveness
&
Reconciliation

Look for these topics in the
Everyday Matters Bible Studies for Women

Forgiveness
&
Reconciliation

Spiritual Practices
FOR EVERYDAY LIFE

HENDRICKSON
PUBLISHERS

**Everyday Matters Bible Studies for Women—
Forgiveness & Reconciliation**

© 2013 by Hendrickson Publishers Marketing, LLC
P.O. Box 3473
Peabody, Massachusetts 01961-3473

ISBN 978-1-61970-146-5

All rights reserved. No part of this book may be reproduced or transmitted in any form or by any means, electronic or mechanical, including photocopying, recording, or by any information storage and retrieval system, without permission in writing from the publisher.

Everyday Matters Bible for Women copyright © 2012 by Hendrickson Publishers. All rights reserved.

Unless otherwise indicated, all Scripture quotations are taken from the Holy Bible, New Living Translation, copyright © 1996, 2004, 2007 by Tyndale House Foundation. Used by permission of Tyndale House Publishers, Inc., Carol Stream, Illinois 60188. All rights reserved.

Printed in the United States of America

Second Printing — June 2014

Contents

Everyday Matters Bible Studies for Women

Reconciliation

Holy Habits

Spiritual Practices for Everyday Life

Everyday life today is busier and more distracting than it has ever been before. While cell phones and texting make it easier to keep track of children and each other, they also make it harder to get away from the demands that overwhelm us. Time, it seems, is a shrinking commodity. But God, the Creator of time, has given us the keys to leading a life that may be challenging but not overwhelming. In fact, he offers us tools to do what seems impossible and come away refreshed and renewed. These tools are called spiritual practices, or spiritual disciplines.

Spiritual practices are holy habits. They are rooted in God's word, and they go back to creation itself. God has hard-wired us to thrive when we obey him, even when it seems like his instructions defy our "common sense." When we engage in the holy habits that God has ordained, time takes on a new dimension. What seems impossible is actually easy; it's easy because we are tapping into God's resources.

The holy habits that we call spiritual practices are all geared to position us in a place where we can allow the Holy Spirit to work in us and through us, to grant us power and strength to do the things we can't do on our own. They take us to a place where we can become intimate with God.

While holy habits and everyday life may sound like opposites, they really aren't.

As you learn to incorporate spiritual practices into your life, you'll find that everyday life is easier. At the same time, you will draw closer to God and come to a place where you can luxuriate in his rich blessings. Here is a simple example. Elizabeth Collings hated running household errands. Picking up dry cleaning, doing the grocery shopping, and chauffeuring her kids felt like a never-ending litany of menial chores. One day she had a simple realization that changed her life. That day she began to use her "chore time" as a time of prayer and fellowship with God.

Whenever Elizabeth walked the aisle of the supermarket, she prayed for each person who would eat the item of food she selected. On her way to pick up her children, she would lay their lives out before God, asking him to be there for them even when she couldn't. Each errand became an opportunity for fellowship with God. The chore that had been so tedious became a precious part of her routine that she cherished.

The purpose of these study guides is to help you use spiritual practices to make your own life richer, fuller, and deeper. The series includes twenty-four spiritual practices that are the building blocks of Christian spiritual formation. Each practice is a "holy habit" that has been modeled for us in the Bible. The practices are acceptance, Bible study and meditation, celebration, community, confession, contemplation, faith, fasting, forgiveness, gratitude, hospitality, justice, mentoring, outreach, prayer, reconciliation, Sabbath and rest, service, silence, simplicity, solitude, stewardship, submission, and worship.

As you move through the practices that you select, remember Christ's promise in Matthew 11:28–30:

> *Come to me, all of you who are weary and carry heavy burdens. Take my yoke upon you. Let me teach you, because I am humble and gentle at heart, and you will find rest for your souls. For my yoke is easy to bear, and the burden I give you is light.*

Introduction

to the Practice of Forgiveness & Reconciliation

What is the hardest thing that God asks of us? Many would argue that it is forgiving those who have unjustly caused us pain or treated us with malice. How do you forgive a friend who has gossiped about you behind your back? A colleague or a boss who has unfairly cost you a raise or a promotion? How does one forgive a spouse who has been unfaithful? Sometimes it just seems like adding insult to injury that you should suffer at the hands of another and then be told to forgive them! And sometimes it feels impossible.

In her article in the *Everyday Matters Bible for Women,* "Forgiving When It Seems Impossible," Dianne Collard recounts the murder of her 23-year-old son Tim. She and her husband were missionaries overseas and were called back to the states because Tim, while doing a friend a favor, had been shot point-blank in the head by an angry stranger. How does a heartbroken mother forgive her son's killer?

Yet the New Testament brims over with story after story of Jesus telling his followers to forgive—not seven times but seventy times seven (Matthew 18:21–22). He doesn't say to forgive those who regret their offense and offer an apology. He doesn't say to forgive some offenses but not others.

The four studies on forgiveness that follow examine some of the challenges we face as we try to obey Christ and forgive those who have hurt us. Because this is such a difficult topic, it merits some preparation before you sit down to begin each study. Here are some things you can do to prepare your heart and your mind in order to get the most out of the material presented:

- Make a list of the people who come to mind whom you haven't forgiven for their offenses.

- Confess to God that you are angry with each one by name. You can be honest with God about your feelings. You probably don't even want to forgive some of the people on your list. God already knows that. Confess your anger anyway.

- Ask him to use your time of study to speak to your heart in a way that will help you move toward forgiveness.

- Return to your list each time you sit down to study one of the lessons and write down anything that has occurred regarding your feelings toward each person.

- Remember that it takes time to forgive, and the greater the offense, the more time it usually takes. Be patient.

One of the stickier Christian practices to which believers are summoned is reconciliation. It is held out as an ideal but is often difficult to achieve in real life. Sometimes reconciliation means advancing to a place that is humanly impossible and unthinkable, as was the case for Hosea when God commanded him to take back his adulterous wife (Hosea 3).

Reconciliation is not just "making up." It also means that when you hear of the pain of those you may consider your enemies, you keep your heart in a posture of sincere sorrow (Proverbs 24). Reconciliation is so difficult, in fact, that only God's power enables true reconciliation. In this way, being reconciled to your brothers and sisters becomes the signature feature that marks one who is "walking in the light."

Reconciliation is part and parcel of forgiving and being forgiven. Is it possible to forgive without reconciliation? Yes, we can forgive someone with our mind, heart, and spirit and still not be reconciled with them. Reconciliation is a mutual action and experience. In order for us to reconcile with someone, that person has to want to reconcile with us. If God had forgiven the children of Israel but they didn't repent or want to be in relationship with him again, reconciliation could not take place. That's true for us, too. Fortunately for us, God *always* wants us to be in relationship with him.

Forgiveness

CHAPTER 1

Why Forgive?

Would You Rather Be Right or Happy?

"And while he was still a long way off, his father saw him coming. Filled with love and compassion, he ran to his son, embraced him, and kissed him."

LUKE 15:20

For this study, read Luke 15:11–31.

Janine had always been the "good daughter" of the family. She was the one who helped out around the house, didn't need to be reminded to do her homework, and never seemed to go through a rebellious teen stage. When as a teen she borrowed the car, her parents never worried about her being reckless or missing her curfew. Her younger sister Susan, however, had always been a handful. She was like a female version of Dennis the Menace: a good kid who meant well but was always getting herself into a jam. When Susan borrowed the car, her parents would hold their collective breath until she pulled back into the driveway.

She was a good kid, but she was a little too reckless for her parents' taste.

No one was surprised when, many years after both girls had grown up and raised their own families, it was Janine who saw to her parents' needs as they grew older and needed help. Susan would occasionally breeze in for brief visits with gifts and entertaining stories, but Janine did the heavy lifting. She made sure her parents had whatever they needed at home. When it became clear that they wouldn't be able to maintain their household much longer, it was Janine and her husband who built a small addition to their home and invited her parents to come live with them. Janine is a lot like the older brother in the parable of the prodigal son. She was steady and responsible; she was there for the long haul, through thick and thin.

The older brother in the parable is often thought of as a killjoy, a jealous sibling who can't rejoice for his father and brother when the family is reunited. A bean counter. The child who can't bear to get one smidgeon less than half of the chocolate bar he has to share with his brother. That's one way to look at it. But it's also true that he's the one who stayed with his father, worked hard and did everything right. Why wouldn't he be angry with his brother, who left him holding the bag and then got a party and a new gold ring from their father when he was pretty much forced to come home? But the parable makes it clear that the older brother should have forgiven his brother. Why?

Occasionally it's easy to forgive; often it's very hard. If we're honest with ourselves, it isn't so hard to see why the older brother was angry with both his brother and his father.

One could argue that the older brother had just lost a big chunk of his half of the chocolate bar. So why should he be forgiving?

The Bible makes it clear that forgiveness and fairness are two different things. In fact, forgiveness is the opposite of fairness or justice. Sounds a lot like mercy, doesn't it?

So why should we forgive? Why does Jesus tell us to forgive our enemies? For their sakes? Perhaps. But it is also for *our* sake. When we harbor anger and resentment, we imprison ourselves in a cell full of poison. In fact, it has been said that being unforgiving toward someone who has hurt you is like taking poison and expecting them to get sick. You may think you're punishing the offender, but you are the one who is paying the price.

We never learn whether or not the older brother attended the party his father threw for his prodigal brother. He may have gone to his room and sulked. Instead of eating fatted calf and drinking fine wine, he might have had cold leftovers.

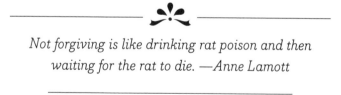

Not forgiving is like drinking rat poison and then waiting for the rat to die. —Anne Lamott

*As you study this chapter, think about situations
in your own life where you feel like you've
been treated unfairly and cannot forgive.*

1. What do you think Jesus wanted his followers to learn
from the story of the prodigal son? In the New Living
Translation, this story is called the "Parable of the Lost
Son." Why do you think the translators used the word "lost"
instead of "prodigal"?

2. Why do you think it is easier to forgive some people than
others? Who is the person in your life you find it most difficult to forgive? What might your relationship look like if
you did forgive that person?

3. What stands out in your memory as a time when you
were forgiven and didn't deserve it?

4. Is there a difference between forgiveness and mercy?

5. Do you need to feel forgiving in order to actually forgive? What does forgiveness look like? What actions can convey forgiveness even when you don't want to forgive?

6. Where would you rather be: at the party or sulking in your room? Would you rather be right or would you rather be happy?

Forgiveness is an act of the will, and the will can function regardless of the temperature of the heart. —Corrie ten Boom

Points to Ponder

*Should we offer him thousands of rams and ten thousand
rivers of olive oil? Should we sacrifice our firstborn children
to pay for our sins? No, O people, the Lord has told you
what is good, and this is what he requires of you: to do what
is right, to love mercy, and to walk humbly with your God.
(Micah 6:7–8)*

• Why do you think God prefers mercy to sacrifice?

• You may have to declare your forgiveness a hundred
times the first day and the second day, but the third
day will be less and each day after, until one day you
will realize you have forgiven completely.
—William Paul Young, *The Shack*

Prayer

Father, you have commanded us to be merciful and to forgive. Please help me to forgive those I don't want to forgive. Please forgive me for my unwillingness to forgive others. Teach me what your mercy looks like.

Add your prayer in your own words.

Amen.

Put It into Practice

Is there someone in your life who needs your forgiveness? This week, take one small step toward forgiving that person. If the matter is not too personal, report back to your group on the step you took and any results that may have occurred since then.

Take-away Treasure

One of the reasons why God commands us to forgive our enemies is because anger corrodes our spirits and makes us unhappy. God wants us to be happy. So if you can't forgive for the other person's sake, then try to forgive for your own sake.

CHAPTER 2

Beyond the Pale

*Are Some Things Just
Too Much to Forgive?*

Purify me from my sins, and I will be clean; wash me,
and I will be whiter than snow. Oh, give me back my
joy again; you have broken me—now let me rejoice.

PSALM 51:7-8

For this study, read 2 Samuel 11:1–12:24.

King David had messed up big time. The situation he addresses in Psalm 51 causes even the most sympathetic reader to wonder what God was thinking when he called David "a man after his own heart" (1 Samuel 13:14). First, David succumbed to physical temptation and brought Bathsheba, another man's wife, to his bed. Worse, when he learned she was pregnant with his child, rather than bravely face the consequences, he orchestrated the demise of her unsuspecting husband, Uriah—who was also one of David's most devoted soldiers. He put Uriah in the front line of battle where he would surely die and did.

The prayer in Psalm 51 is an appropriate and wrenching confession before God in the aftermath of two deeds that make the *two-of-the-worst-things-a-human-can-do* list. Even though David was a man after God's own heart, he committed some heinous, cowardly, and devious sins. After David realized how terribly he had sinned, he was distraught and penitent. And God ultimately forgave him, but not before he had exacted a punishment for David's sin. While forgiveness is always available from God, there are often real consequences that follow from our wrong actions. David and Bathsheba's child died, as God said he would. That's not the end of the story, though. Bathsheba went on to bear another son of David: Solomon, who would be one of Israel's greatest kings. Part of God's amazing love and forgiveness is that even when our lives feel like ashes, God gives us beauty and joy.

For his unfailing love toward those who fear him is as great as the height of the heavens above the earth. He has removed our sins as far from us as the east is from the west. The Lord is like a father to his children, tender and compassionate to those who fear him. (Psalm 103:11–12)

> **As you study this chapter, remember**
> **that there is nothing God can't or won't**
> **forgive. He asks us to do the same.**

1. Do you recall the circumstances that caused David to confront these sins for what they were? The prophet Nathan came to him with a sad story (told as a parable in 1 Samuel 12) that elicited David's indignation. Nathan turned the story around to show David how he himself was the story's culprit, which shocked David. What does this suggest about the nature of confronting our own sin?

2. Read Psalm 51. In this gut-wrenching confession, David seems to hold nothing back in crying to God about his shame. Even so, his confession misses a few particular concrete elements he did not articulate. Why do you think David omitted them? What is the value of "coming clean" when we confess our sins?

3. When David confessed his sin against God to Nathan, the prophet assured him he was forgiven. First John 1:9 says, "But if we confess our sins to him, he is faithful and just to forgive us our sins and to cleanse us from all wickedness." What are some of the practical benefits of confessing our sins to God? To the person we have sinned against?

4. Bathsheba's husband Uriah was killed and her newborn child died. Yet we don't learn anything about her responses to all that happened in this story. How do you imagine she felt? If Bathsheba were to tell this story, how do you think she'd relate it? Do you think she was angry with David?

5. While the child that Bathsheba bore died shortly after its birth, Bathsheba went on to give birth to Solomon, who is known even today for his extraordinary wisdom. Is there a situation in your life where God allowed something wonderful to come out of something that was conceived in sin?

6. Have you or someone you know been hurt by infidelity? Have you asked God to forgive the offender? Are you willing to?

To be Christian means to forgive the inexcusable because God has forgiven the inexcusable in you. —C. S. Lewis

Points to Ponder

- In God's graciousness and forgiveness, he often allows good to flow from what started out as evil. Perhaps in your own life, you can forgive someone's offense and go on to experience good things in that relationship despite the hardship and hurt.

- David could easily have been so angry with himself for his horrific behavior that he might have given up on his relationship with God. How would history have been different had David not forgiven himself?

Prayer

Dear Lord and Father, we have sinned against you. We have sinned against one another. Thank you for your eternal forgiveness of those who confess their sins to you and repent of them.

Please forgive me for . . .

Amen.

Put It into Practice

In the Lord's Prayer, Jesus prayed, "Forgive us our sins, as we have forgiven those who sin against us" (Matthew 6:12). This week, take the first step toward forgiving someone who has sinned against you. It may be as simple as asking God to help you forgive the offender; it may be trying to under-stand what it is in that person that caused her to stumble; it may be taking a plate of homemade cookies to her even though she doesn't deserve that kindness. Just take one step.

Take-away Treasure

If you are feeling like your life is in ashes, ask God for beauty and joy. Remember, you are on a journey and God is faithful. You don't know the end of the story yet.

CHAPTER 3

Pay It Forward

Has Anyone Ever Forgiven You?

> "But the man fell down before his master and
> begged him, 'Please, be patient with me, and I will
> pay it all.' Then his master was filled with pity for
> him, and he released him and forgave his debt."
>
> MATTHEW 18:26-27

For this study, read Matthew 18:21–35.

Some of the parables Jesus told are harder to untangle than
others, and the parable of the unforgiving debtor is one
of the toughest. At first it seems pretty straightforward: a
servant has borrowed a tremendous amount of money from
the king. When the debt comes due, the servant throws
himself before the king and begs for more time to repay the
money. The king is filled with pity for the poor man and
forgives the debt entirely.

If that was the end of the story, it would be a heartwarm-
ing tale, but it wouldn't be a parable. The story goes on.
That same servant who was just forgiven a huge debt (the
New Living Translation tells us that the man owed the king

millions of dollars!) goes straight to a colleague who owes him money and demands payment in full. The man pleads with him, saying exactly what the servant had just told the king: "Be patient with me, and I will pay it." Despite the fact that he had just been forgiven his own debt, the lender has his debtor thrown in prison.

When the king hears about the incident, he calls in the man he had just forgiven and has him thrown in prison and tortured "until he had paid his entire debt" (v. 34). Then Jesus says something chilling: "That's what my heavenly Father will do to you if you refuse to forgive your brothers and sisters from your heart." Those are tough words. It sounds like unforgiveness is one of the things that angers God most.

As we've said, forgiving someone who has wronged us is one of the most difficult challenges we face. But clearly it is important for us to pursue. When we remember all the times we've been forgiven, certainly by God and also by other people, it is easier to forgive (though not easy) by looking at it as "paying it forward."

*Forgiveness is not about forgetting. It is about
letting go of another person's throat.*
—*William Paul Young*, The Shack

*As you study this chapter, think about the
times you have either forgiven someone else
or needed to forgive them and couldn't. Does
the idea of "paying it forward" help you?*

1. Today's study starts out with Peter asking Jesus how often to forgive. He asks if seven times is enough. Jesus says, "No, not seven times, but seventy times seven." Have you ever had to forgive someone over and over again? Does it get easier? Why do you think Jesus followed up with this particular parable?

2. At first, the king ordered that his servant be sold (along with his family and possessions) in order to pay the debt. What caused him to relent and forgive the debt instead? Do you think his response would have been different if the servant denied owing him money? What is the value of acknowledging our guilt when we are truly in the wrong?

3. The servant who demanded payment from his colleague probably felt justified in requiring that the money owed him be paid despite the fact that he had just been forgiven his own debt. He probably needed his money back; after all, he was just a servant. In the parable, does that seem to matter? What is the lesson here?

4. Do we have to "feel" forgiving in order to actually forgive? Is forgiveness a feeling or is it a decision?

5. At first, the king ordered that the servant and his family be sold. After the servant refused to forgive the man who owed him money, the king ordered that the servant to thrown into prison and tortured until the entire debt was paid. This seems like far worse punishment than the original one. Why do you think the king increased the punishment?

6. In verse 35, Jesus says we must forgive our brothers and sisters from our heart. Why do you think he included the words "from your heart"? Is that for the sake of the offender or for our sake?

Points to Ponder

- In his article "Understanding Forgiveness" in the *Everyday Matters Bible for Women,* Lewis Smedes says that the first thing required in forgiveness is that "we surrender our right to get even." Is there a situation in your life where you can surrender your right to get even? Will you try?

- Dr. Smedes also says that forgiving from the heart takes time. In other words, we often have to forgive the same offender over and over again. Who are you trying to forgive? Will you try more than once?

As I walked out the door toward the gate that would lead to my freedom, I knew that if I didn't leave my bitterness and hatred behind, I'd still be in prison. —Nelson Mandela

Prayer

Almighty God, our Heavenly Father, you have made it clear in your word that it is important to you that we forgive. Sometimes it seems impossible to do so. Please give me extra portions of your grace and your mercy so I may pay them forward to those who have wronged me.

Add your prayer in your own words.

Amen.

Put It into Practice

- *People are often unreasonable and self-centered. Forgive them anyway.*

- *If you are kind, people may accuse you of ulterior motives. Be kind anyway.*

- *If you are honest, people may cheat you. Be honest anyway.*

- *If you find happiness, people may be jealous. Be happy anyway.*

- *The good you do today may be forgotten tomorrow. Do good anyway.*

- *Give the world the best you have and it may never be enough. Give your best anyway.*

- *For you see, in the end, it is between you and God. It was never between you and them anyway.*

—Mother Teresa

Take-away Treasure

"Remember," says Lewis Smedes, "God does not expect *perfect* forgiving; he is the only expert at it. We're just poor, imperfect sinners trying our hardest to treat others as he treats us."

CHAPTER 4

Get Over It

Moving Beyond Resentment

Jesus said, "Father; forgive them, for they
don't know what they are doing."

LUKE 23:34

For this study, read Luke 23:32–43.

Ruby Bridges was 6 years old, just starting school in her
hometown of New Orleans. The year was 1960, and the
Supreme Court had outlawed school segregation. For the
first time in the South, schools were being forced to admit
African-American children. Six first graders were chosen to
integrate the city's school system, and Ruby Bridges was the
only black child starting at her school that day. Ruby, accompanied by federal marshals, walked up the school steps
past a mob of angry protesters who were waving their fists
and screaming threats and obscenities. One woman even
brought a black doll in a small wooden coffin and held it out
in front of Ruby as she tried to get to the school.

The little girl stopped and talked to some of the people who were protesting. When asked what she had said, Ruby answered that she wasn't talking to them; she was praying. "I prayed that I would be strong and not afraid. And I prayed for my enemies, that God would forgive them. Jesus prayed that on the cross; 'Forgive them, because they don't know what they're doing.'"

Ruby's ordeal didn't end that first day of school. Ongoing threats to poison her—even to kill her—made it impossible for Ruby to join in with the other children at recess and lunch. When she had to use the bathroom, federal marshals accompanied her down the hall and back to the classroom. Parents pulled their children out of the school and teachers refused to teach her. Ruby's ordeal lasted for a full year.

One might expect Ruby to become angry and resentful. But her life's story shows that she escaped being imprisoned by resentment. Ruby went on to enjoy a strong marriage and a successful career. She and her husband raised four sons, and in 1999 she formed the Ruby Bridges Foundation to promote the values of tolerance, respect, and appreciation of differences.

In her excellent article "Moving beyond Resentment" in the *Everyday Matters Bible for Women,* Frederica Mathewes-Green says, "In reality our opponents are not our enemies. We have an Enemy, who wants to destroy both our opponent and us. . . . There is only one way to defeat him: to love our enemies instead." Perhaps if in the face of offense we were to pray, "Father, forgive her, because she doesn't know what she's doing," we would escape resentment, which hurts us far more than it hurts anyone else.

*With each opportunity before me, God presented me
with a choice. I could accept his offerings, His wisdom,
His grace. Or I could choose to hold onto the pain,
the anger and the resentment a little longer.*
—Sharon E. Rainey, Making a Pearl from the Grit of Life

**As you study this chapter, think about
ways you can "love your enemy."**

1. In today's reading, Jesus is mocked, robbed, and tortured.
What does he mean when he prays to the Father that "they
don't know what they're doing"? What do you think Ruby
meant when she said the same thing of her tormenters? Do
you think they all really *knew* what they were doing or was
any ignorance involved?

2. Throughout the New Testament, Jesus repeats his com-
mand to forgive (see Matthew 6:12, Mark 11:25, Luke 17:4).
Why do you think this is such a pervasive theme throughout his ministry and teaching? Is forgiving for the sake of
the perpetrator or the person who has been hurt?

3. In his article on forgiveness in the *Everyday Matters Bible for Women*, Lewis Smedes says that in forgiving we must "wish our wrongdoer well." Is it possible to wish well the person who has hurt you and still harbor resentment?

4. One of the three Greek words usually translated as "forgive" in the New Testament actually means "to release, to hurl away, to free yourself from something" (see "Throwing Away Resentment" by Allen Guelzo in the *Everyday Matters Bible for Women*). If you were to hurl away an offense, do you think resentment would ensue?

5. Is there someone in your life you resent? How much of your energy have you used feeling that resentment? Could that energy have been better spent—and more gratifying—elsewhere?

6. No one ever said it is easy to let go of resentment; it is one of the hardest thing we'll ever do. What steps can you take to let go of resentment? This week, pray at least once every day for one person you resent. At the end of the week, think about whether you feel any different toward that person.

Hanging on to resentment is letting someone who has hurt you live rent-free inside your head. —Ann Landers

Points to Ponder

- It is often said that "hurting people hurt other people." Think about people who have hurt you. Are they hurting? Were they hurt early in their lives? Do they carry scars that cause them to hurt others?

- In Ephesians 4:26–27, Paul says, "Don't let the sun go down while you are still angry, for anger gives a foothold to the devil." Have you ever noticed that the longer you're angry, the more intense your anger becomes? If you resent someone today, try to follow Paul's advice in this passage and get it resolved before tonight. Tell your study group the results next week.

Prayer

Dear Lord, I confess to you today that I am holding on to resentment against _____. Please heal me of the feelings I harbor. Please bless_____ today in all that he/she does. Forgive me my sins against you and help me to forgive the sins that _____ has committed against me. I pray for a renewed spirit of generosity. Please help me to give _____ the benefit of the doubt. In the name of your Son Jesus.

Add your prayer in your own words.

Amen.

Put It into Practice

This week, write the name of a person you still resent on a slip of paper. Hold the paper in your hand as you pray for that person and for your ability to let go of your resentment. Then crumple up the paper and toss it in the trash. Later, if you think of the resentment, remember that you threw it away.

Take-away Treasure

If you hug to yourself any resentment against anybody else, you destroy the bridge by which God would come to you.
—*Peter Marshall*

Notes / Prayer Requests

Notes / Prayer Requests

Reconciliation

CHAPTER 1

Reconciling with God

The Story of Redeeming Love

> Then the Lord said to me, "Go and love your wife
> again, even though she commits adultery with
> another lover. This will illustrate that the Lord
> still loves Israel, even though the people have
> turned to other gods and love to worship them."
>
> HOSEA 3:1

For this study, read Hosea 1:1–3:5.

In Francine Rivers' best-selling novel *Redeeming Love*, she uses the book of Hosea as the basis for a poignant story about Michael Hosea, a good man who rescues a woman who has been forced into a life of prostitution. She has the face of an angel and a heart of stone. Over and over again, she tries to return to her old life, and each time Michael patiently goes after her, forgiving her for unspeakable acts of betrayal, anger, and hostility. His tender love for her seems impossible.

This story mirrors the Old Testament account of the prophet Hosea, whom God instructed to marry a prostitute.

Hosea's life with his wife Gomer becomes a symbol of God's love for his adulterous people, the children of Israel, and his willingness to restore them to their standing as the chosen people. It is a vivid picture of Yahweh tenderly wooing them back into relationship with him.

In Rivers' novel, Michael Hosea's prostitute wife Angel is not a likable character. Though she is physically stunningly beautiful, her ugly, hateful behavior toward her husband makes the reader wonder why he doesn't just walk away. In Hosea 3, the writer describes Israel's "period of probation." Similarly, while Hosea takes back his adulterous wife despite her infidelity and breach of trust, Gomer's transgressions must be reckoned with and repented of before there can be reconciliation. Repentance, a prominent theme in Hosea, precedes reconciliation.

Before we reconcile with anyone else, we need to be sure we're reconciled with God—not only in terms of salvation, but also in terms of our current relationship with him.

Forgiving and being reconciled to our enemies or our loved ones are not about pretending that things are other than they are. . . . True reconciliation exposes the truth. It is a risky undertaking but in the end it is worthwhile, because in the end only an honest confrontation with reality can bring real healing. Superficial reconciliation can bring only superficial healing. —Desmond Tutu

> *As you study this chapter, ask God if
> there is anything in your life that is
> hindering your relationship with him.*

1. As you focus on reconciliation with God, does the story of Hosea make you identify with any of the behaviors of the Israelites? Are you currently reconciled with God? Do you think our sins cause God sorrow? What actions of the people of God today might equal the adulterous behaviors of the people of Israel? Are you guilty of any? Have you had to forgive any?

2. One of the sins that infuriates and hurts God most is when his people worship other gods (see Hosea 9:1). What other gods do many of us worship today? Are you unwittingly worshipping any other gods? How can you take steps to cut them down to size?

3. In Hosea and in the Old Testament in general, God exacted serious punishment on his people before reconciliation could take place. Is this a function of the fact that the Messiah had not yet come, or do you believe that God punishes his wayward children today?

4. This brief but dramatic story demonstrates the heroic measures reconciliation often requires: action, initiative, communication, and forgiveness. God took action and initiative both in confronting the Israelites with the truth of their behavior and in calling them back to him. Is there someone who has offended you who needs to be confronted with the truth of their behavior in order to start the process of reconciliation? Is it possible to confront someone else without displaying hostility? Is there someone who needs to forgive you? Are you willing to start the process yourself?

5. Read 2 Corinthians 5:16–21. Verse 19 says, "For God was in Christ, reconciling the world to himself, no longer counting people's sins against them. And he gave us this wonderful message of reconciliation." Whether we like to admit it or not, sometimes we get satisfaction in holding onto someone's sin against us. Are there people in your life whose offenses you should stop counting against them?

6. In her article on racial reconciliation in the *Everyday Matters Bible for Women*, Brenda Salter McNeil says that reconciliation with God forms the vertical axis of the cross, and reconciliation with one another forms the horizontal axis of the cross, allowing us to become people of the cross. We think of reconciliation in terms of individuals, but it also applies across ethnic, gender, cultural, and economic divisions. Does your body of believers work toward reconciliation in any of these areas? Is there a particular issue in the life of your church or community that calls out for this sort of reconciliation? Are you willing to start the ball rolling?

*Forgiveness in no way requires that you trust the one
you forgive. But should they finally confess and repent,
you will discover a miracle in your own heart that allows
you to reach out and begin to build between you a bridge
of reconciliation.* —William Paul Young, The Shack

Points to Ponder

- Did you know that Australia has an annual event called National Sorry Day? It is meant to commemorate the mistreatment of the continent's indigenous population. Consider instituting a Sorry Day in your household. Sometimes one "I'm sorry" is worth a bushel of debate.

- Hannah Whiteall Smith said, "Look upon your chastening as God's chariots sent to carry your soul to the high places of spiritual achievement." If God is chastening you, remember that his sole motive is his love for you and his desire for you to move onto higher planes of blessing.

Prayer

Dear Lord, thank you for constantly wanting to reconcile with your errant children. Thank you for taking the first step through the sacrifice of your Son. I ask your forgiveness for any way that I have strayed from you. If I am holding onto offenses—my own and others'—please give me the desire and ability to release them and open up the channel for reconciliation. Forgive me my sins and help me to forgive those who have sinned against me.

Add your prayer in your own words.

Amen.

Put It into Practice

If you are in a broken relationship right now, think about the points of struggle that have brought about the strain. Ask God to reveal aspects of your own disposition that may contribute to the problem. Write down areas where you desire to grow and pray through them. Then write down the aspects of the offending party's conduct that have hurt you and pray for them.

Take-away Treasure

It is difficult to practice reconciliation. But even small gestures can initiate healing. Today, do something small!

CHAPTER 2

Reconciling with Yourself

Are You Ever Your Own Worst Enemy?

> Jesus replied, "The most important commandment is this: 'Listen, O Israel! The Lord our God is the one and only Lord. And you must love the Lord your God with all your heart, all your soul, all your mind, and all your strength.' The second is equally important: 'Love your neighbor as yourself.' No other commandment is greater than these."
>
> MARK 12:29-31

For this study, read Mark 12:28–34.

When we think of reconciliation, we usually think of reconciling with another person. But the biblical passage above, short as it is, reveals something *huge* we often overlook: We can only love others as much as we love ourselves. This truth is both freeing and terrifying, because so many of us don't truly love ourselves.

Josie is a gracious, delightful woman who makes friends easily and thinks nothing of putting herself out to help others. She tells of an experience she had several years ago that stopped her in her tracks. She had just started a new job that was several notches higher than the one she'd left. She had to learn a lot of new skills in a short amount of time in order to do the job well, and she was having trouble understanding some of the things she needed to master.

Josie found herself sitting at her desk unable to do a thing. She was paralyzed by fear. What if she wasn't up to the task? What if she lost her job? She started criticizing herself for ever thinking in the first place that she could handle such a big job. "You're just a big impostor," she heard herself think. Soon the voice inside her head was telling her that she was incompetent, lazy, and a fake. There she sat, unable to do a stitch of work and feeling like a horrible person.

At one point, a thought occurred to her: "If you saw a friend sitting in her office suffering like you are, how would you respond?" She thought that she would feel terrible for her friend and want to help and encourage her. Her next thought was: "What if that person was someone you don't really know?" She knew she would feel sorry for the person even if she didn't feel comfortable offering help. Then the final question that came to mind was, "What if that person was someone who has treated you horribly? Someone who was a real enemy?" Josie decided that even while she might not feel very kindly toward the person, she would still feel some sympathy for them.

The final thought that she had was this: "So if you just treated yourself as well as you treat your worst enemy, you'd be better off than you are now."

What a concept! Josie was stunned by the odd internal con-versation that had just occurred in her mind. She realized that she was harder on herself than on anyone else, that she was unable to extend to herself even a small bit of kindness or compassion. In other words, she didn't really love herself.

Josie is a Christian, and she believes the Holy Spirit was prompting her to have that conversation with herself. She was shocked into realizing that there was something terribly wrong with her attitude toward herself. She started studying the Scriptures to learn what the Bible has to say about the subject, and today's verse was utterly pivotal for her. *Love your neighbor as you love yourself.*

I think that if God forgives us we must forgive ourselves.
Otherwise, it is almost like setting up ourselves
as a higher tribunal than Him. —C. S. Lewis

As you study through this chapter, think of
ways you can be kinder toward yourself.

1. Do you love yourself? Are you as kind to yourself as you are to others? If not, you are disobeying what Jesus calls one of the two most important commandments in the Bible.

2. Read 1 Corinthians 4–7. This passage is often read at weddings and we think of it in the context of loving others. When you read the passage, think about yourself as the beloved.

3. What behaviors are you told to exhibit toward yourself? Are there any you need to work on?

4. Sometimes we confuse love with indulgence. In your own life, what are some of the differences between truly loving yourself and simply indulging yourself?

5. Sometimes love needs to be tough love. What are some areas in your life that merit some tough love from you? For example, do you take proper care of your health? Do you get proper exercise and nourishment? Do you carve out enough time for yourself? If the answer is no, think about how you will address those issues.

6. Guilt corrodes love, both for others and for oneself. If you are feeling guilty about something, and if that guilt is the conviction of the Holy Spirit, how can you resolve the issue? This might involve righting a wrong you committed long ago, or it might be as simple as acknowledging your role in a disagreement. Whatever it is, God wants to give you the strength and stamina you need in order to resolve it.

7. God loves you, so if you don't love yourself, what does that say about God?

It is in pardoning that we are pardoned.
—*St. Francis of Assisi*

Points to Ponder

- Henry Ward Beecher said that an offense that's been forgiven ought to be like a cancelled I.O.U.—torn up and burned so it can never be used against the offender. When you are tempted to remind yourself of your own failings and shortcomings, after you have confessed and repented, tear up and burn the memories of them.

- Speaking about the Beatitudes, John Piper said that when Moses protested to God that he was not eloquent, God didn't say to him, "Stop putting yourself down! Of course you're eloquent." No, God said to Moses, "Stop looking at your unworthiness and look at me. I will be with you. I will help you." Will you, when you feel inadequate, ask God to help you?

Prayer

Heavenly Father, thank you that you love me so much
that you gave your Son to die for me. I confess that
I have not loved you with my whole heart. I have not
loved my neighbor as myself. I haven't even loved myself properly. Please help me to remember that since
you have forgiven me, I am now free to forgive myself,
and help me to do it.

Add your prayer in your own words.

Amen.

Put It into Practice

This week, write yourself a letter of love and reconciliation.
Make a list of the ways in which you do not accept or properly love yourself. Then pray every day for healing in one of
those areas until you've covered every item on the list.

Take-away Treasure

If the God of the universe loves you (and he does!), then
who are you not to do the same?

CHAPTER 3

Reconciling with Your Enemy

Clues from the Beatitudes

"God blesses those who are merciful,
for they will be shown mercy.
God blesses those whose hearts are pure,
for they will see God.
God blesses those who work for peace,
for they will be called the children of God."

MATTHEW 5:7-9

For this study, read Matthew 5:1–12.

This week's reading is the portion of Christ's Sermon on the Mount known as the Beatitudes. It has been said that these are *attitudes* that should *be* in the life of every child of God. Jesus starts each beatitude by saying, "God blesses . . ." or, in the King James Version, "Blessed are . . ." The Greek term "blessed" means "happy," "fortunate," and "favored." So Jesus is saying that we are happy when we are merciful, happy when our hearts are pure, and happy when we work for peace.

It's easy to think of someone being happy when they're working for world peace, but working for peace with someone who has wronged you or with whom your relationship is broken doesn't sound like a happy process. It sounds difficult.

Perhaps that's why Christ talked about those who are merciful and whose hearts are pure before bringing up the idea of making peace. First, we need to possess a merciful attitude. Without mercy, peace is hard to come by. Next, we need to have a pure heart or pure intentions. When we truly want to reconcile with another, we need to want it for the right reasons. It seems like the common element in these—and in the other beatitudes—is the willingness to let go. We need to let go of the need to be right; we need to let go of any hidden motives. But look at what we get in return: we will be shown mercy; we will see God; we will be called God's children.

We may not be able to prevent other people from being our enemies, but we can prevent ourselves from being enemies toward others. —*Warren Wiersbe*

*As you study this chapter, meditate
on the Beatitudes and what they mean
(or should mean) in your life.*

1. In your experience, whom (no need to discuss names) might you deem an enemy? Examine your heart to see if you possess a spirit that would truly be grieved to learn of their hardship or failure.

2. If you've found that you don't have a spirit of compassion toward your enemies, in what way can you begin to change?

3. Have you considered that someone you know might consider you an enemy? If so, who? Are you willing to be a peacemaker with them?

4. So much that happens in today's world is unjust, and reconciliation is often beyond our normal human inclinations. Why do you think God calls his people to live this way?

5. The last group of people Jesus mentions in the Beatitudes are those who are mocked and persecuted because they are his followers. It is that group he specifically says should be happy because a great reward awaits them in heaven. Why do you think this group is at the end of his list?

6. Read through verses 1–12 once more. This time think of the "blessed" as "happy." Now do it again and think of them as "fortunate." Do you feel happy or fortunate when you're feeling poor or are mourning or persecuted?

*Don't rejoice when your enemies fall; don't be
happy when they stumble. For the Lord will
be displeased with you and will turn his anger
away from them. Don't fret because of evildoers;
don't envy the wicked. (Proverbs 24:17–19)*

Points to Ponder

Oswald Chambers said, "Get alone with Jesus and either tell
Him you do not want sin to die out in you—or else tell Him
that at all costs you want to be identified with His death."

- Which will you choose?

- What will this require of you?

Prayer

Lord, when my heart beats quickly and my mind feels
unsettled because of the actions of someone else, touch
me in a special way that settles my soul and fills me
with your peace.

Add your prayer in your own words.

Amen.

Put It into Practice

When you are doing physical exercise or running an errand—
anything that takes you outside of your emotions—get into
the habit of praying for people who have harmed you. It's best
to do it when you have something else that keeps you moving. You'll find, in time, that it gets easier.

Take-away Treasure

In Psalm 23:6, David says that "goodness and unfailing love
will pursue me all the days of my life." God has sent you unfailing love for your whole life. Remember to use it!

CHAPTER 4

The Secret

Doing the Impossible

"You have heard the law that says, 'Love your
neighbor' and hate your enemy. But I say, love
your enemies! Pray for those who persecute
you! In that way, you will be acting as true
children of your Father in heaven. For he gives
his sunlight to both the evil and the good, and
he sends rain on the just and the unjust alike."

MATTHEW 5:43-45

For this study, read Matthew 5:43–48.

Love your enemies! Pray for those who persecute you!

Is he kidding? Next thing you know he'll be telling us to be
willing to shed blood for our enemies. Oh wait. He did that.
In fact, Jesus did all three.

When Jesus told us to love our enemies and to pray for
those who persecute us, he was introducing strange new
ideas of what it means to belong to God's family. In fact,
these were new and revolutionary terms. No longer was

obedience to God measured in the Old Testament law and a system of rituals. Jesus established new principles that make *greater* demands on God's followers.

Think about it. It is *easier* not to commit murder (as in the Old Testament) than it is not to show anger toward a brother or sister, as Jesus outlines here. Many would say that Jesus is asking the impossible. In fact, he is.

By asking us—by *commanding* us—to do the impossible, Jesus renders every member of his Kingdom helpless. Everyone is in need of God's grace. Jesus annihilates all religious hierarchies and social class. This section of his teaching is revolutionary and unmatched among any religious teachers of his time or since.

How do we do the impossible? How do we love our enemies? How do we reconcile with our enemies, which doesn't allow us to love them from afar? The answer is deceptively simple: We can do it only by the grace of God.

In Jesus and for Him, enemies and friends alike are to be loved. —Thomas à Kempis

> *As you study this chapter, think about those who have hurt you and how you can, through God's grace, respond with his love.*

1. Jesus' exhortation to love one's enemies clearly reaches beyond what is possible by human standards. Why would he uphold such an unreasonable standard for those desiring to be called children of God?

2. What does Jesus mean when he says God gives sunlight to the evil and the good? What does this have to do with reconciliation?

3. Reconciliation can be a delicate matter. Is it possible to be reconciled with someone who has not repented of her wrongdoing against you?

4. Do you think it is possible to experience reconciliation without resolution? In other words, can true reconciliation take place under the notion that two parties "agree to disagree"? Have you experienced this?

5. In the Gospels, Jesus frequently says the opposite of what one would expect: love those who hate you; the last shall be first; he came to earth to bring not peace but a sword. Why do you think he turned logic upside down so often in his teachings?

6. In Matthew 6:45, Jesus says that God sends the sunlight and rain to the good and evil, the just and the unjust. What does that have to do with the rest of this study's passage?

Points to Ponder

May God, who gives this patience and encouragement, help you live in complete harmony with each other, as is fitting for followers of Christ Jesus. (Romans 15:5)

• Think of ways you can "live in complete harmony" with others.

• What needs to change in your life and in your attitude?

Prayer

Lord, the challenge is daunting to pray for those who are actively hostile toward me. Give me the habit of praying for my enemies, even if the feelings in my heart have not reached conformity to this habit. In time, please change my heart to equal the habit.

Add your prayer in your own words.

Amen.

Put It into Practice

Each day when you look upon the landscape of your life for that day, think about a person or situation that is a source of antagonism. Consciously pray about this, using specific language, and pray to the center of your pain, asking God to enter it.

Take-away Treasure

Remember that much of the time people who hurt us are in pain themselves. If someone is hurting you, think about the reasons why she might be in pain and try to put yourself in her place. Can you relate to her on any level?

Notes / Prayer Requests

_____

_____

_____

_____

_____

_____

_____

_____

_____

_____

_____

_____

_____

_____

_____

_____

_____

_____

_____

Notes / Prayer Requests

Leader's Guide

to Forgiveness & Reconciliation

Thoughts on Where to Meet

- If you have the chance, encourage each group member to host a gathering. But make sure your host knows that you don't expect fresh baked scones from scratch or white-glove-test-worthy surroundings. Set the tone for a relaxed and open atmosphere with a warm welcome wherever you can meet. The host can provide the space and the guests can provide the goodies.

- If you can't meet in homes, consider taking at least one of your meetings on the road. Can you meet at a local place where people from your community gather? A park or a coffee shop or other public space perhaps.

- If you meet in a church space, consider partnering with another local church group and take turns hosting. How can you extend your welcome outside your group?

Thoughts on Ways to Foster Welcome

- If many of your members have a hard time meeting due to circumstances, look for ways to work around it. Consider providing childcare if there are moms who have difficulty attending, or meet in an accessible space if someone who might want to join has a disability. Does a morning time work better? Could you meet as smaller groups and then get together as a larger group for an event? Be flexible and see how you can accommodate the needs of the group. Incorporate "get to know you" activities to promote sharing. Don't take yourselves too seriously and let your humor shine through.

Incorporating Other Practices

- *Lift your voices.* Integrate worship throughout the study. Find songs that speak about forgiveness and reconciliation.

- *Commit to lift each other up in prayer.* You may want to have a prayer walk as part of seeing opportunities to serve in your community, or prayer partners who might be able to meet at other times.

- *Dig deep into the word.* Take the study at your own pace but consider including passages for participants to read in between meetings. The *Everyday Matters Bible for Women* has a wealth of additional resources.

- *Give thanks.* Gratitude reenergizes us for humble service. Assemble a group list of one hundred reasons to give thanks.

Forgiveness

Chapter 1: Ask each member of the group which brother in the parable of the prodigal son they most relate to—the younger brother or the older? Ask one person who identifies with the older brother to role-play a conversation acting as the younger brother; ask one who identifies with the younger brother to do the same with the older brother. Ask them to discuss their feelings about the situation described in the parable in front of the group. Afterwards, discuss with the group any of their feelings and thoughts that might have surprised them as they listened or participated in the exchange. Did anything change for any of the group members?

Chapter 2: David's adultery and his orchestration of Uriah's killing on the battlefield are heinous sins, and hopefully no one in your group has personal experience with either! But this story could definitely bring intense feelings to the surface if a group member does relate to any of it. Gently ask if anyone cares to share any difficult responses she might have had as she studied this lesson. Remember that this study is about forgiveness. You might want to discuss in this session how difficult it can be to forgive a horrific betrayal such as David's. Ask the group why it is important for someone who has been terribly hurt to forgive. Is it in order to help the perpetrator or the victim? Remember that your session is not about giving one another advice; stick to the Scriptures!

Chapter 3: The Scripture passage assigned for today's study (Matthew 18:21–35) starts out with Peter asking Jesus how often he should forgive someone, and Jesus answers "seventy times seven." Theologians have remarked that this is a way of saying, "Forgive everybody for everything all of the time," since by the time you get to 490 you might as well stop counting! Discuss with the group the concept of *forgiving everybody for everything all the time.* It sounds utterly impossible, but it must not be if Jesus says to do it. What is the value of obeying that exhortation? (Hint: Think of all the time, energy, and peace of mind we waste by not forgiving everybody everything all the time.) Ask each member of the group to be especially mindful in the coming week of times they feel angry, hurt, unforgiving, or resentful. When they do feel that way, ask them to say to themselves, "Forgive everybody for everything all the time." Next week, ask if there were any interesting results from that exercise.

Chapter 4: Today's lesson discusses Christ's final experiences during his crucifixion as well as those of little Ruby Bridges. Have any members of the group had their own "crucifixion experience" in which they were hurt or abused in a way that was extraordinarily hurtful or had lasting effects? Ask if anyone wants to discuss their experience. While forgiveness of serious offenses can feel impossible, small steps can lead to healing. Ask the group to review some of the steps that have been discussed in the sessions that might help the member(s) get further along the right path.

While this is the last session in this study on forgiveness, the problem of anger and resentment rarely takes a vacation. Your group should find the next study on reconciliation helpful in continuing this discussion of forgiveness. If you feel your group needs even more time with the subject of forgiveness, consider using the *Everyday Matters Bible for Women*'s articles and profiles on the topic for further discussion. An index at the back of the Bible provides references for all of the spiritual practices.

Reconciliation

Chapter 1: Francine Rivers was a best-selling romance novelist when she became a believer, and *Redeeming Love* was the first novel she wrote after she was won to Christ. After more than twenty years, it is her best-selling book with millions of copies sold. Does the group think there might be a connection between that fact and Rivers' own experience of reconciliation with God? What lessons might be in that? If your group hasn't read the book, consider doing so while you study reconciliation.

Chapter 2: Learning to love ourselves is particularly difficult for many women. One might think that as Christians, it would be easier to do that. Discussing this topic honestly may be difficult for people as they consider their own lives. Why does the group think this is such a big issue among Christians? Discuss some specific ways that members can help one another in this area.

At the beginning of this session, ask group members to bow their heads and use a minute of silence to think about their own issues with loving themselves, praying for the special presence of the Holy Spirit to speak to their particular challenges in this area and to provide insight and healing. After a moment, lead in a short prayer.

Chapter 3: After you've discussed this week's reading and questions, ask someone to read aloud Luke 6:20–23. This is the second account in the Gospels of Jesus' delivery of the Beatitudes. Are there any differences in this account from the one in Matthew? Why are they not identical? Is there any meaning in this or was it just a difference in Luke's perception?

Chapter 4: This chapter continues with the notion of Jesus' counterintuitive teachings—of which there are many—on love, forgiveness, and reconciliation. What other passages and scenarios in the Gospels include his messages on these two topics? Why does the group think that Christ spoke so much more often about these topics in his ministry than others?

Since this is the final group meeting of these two disciplines, ask each member what spoke to her most as she studied over these four (or eight) weeks. Is there anything that has changed in her life as a result of her study? Is there a particular area that members can pray about on her behalf in the coming weeks and months? Share your story and request first. Be as open and transparent as possible. This will set the tenor for the whole discussion.

EVERYDAY MATTERS BIBLE STUDIES
for women

Spiritual practices for everyday life

Acceptance	Mentoring
Bible Study & Meditation	Outreach
Celebration	Prayer
Community	Reconciliation
Confession	Sabbath & Rest
Contemplation	Service
Faith	Silence
Fasting	Simplicity
Forgiveness	Solitude
Gratitude	Stewardship
Hospitality	Submission
Justice	Worship

HENDRICKSON PUBLISHERS

"It's fresh, it's new, and it's invigorating..."

—DEBBIE EATON, Saddleback Church, Director of Women's Ministry

everyday matters

BIBLE *for women*

Buy today at your favorite bookstore!

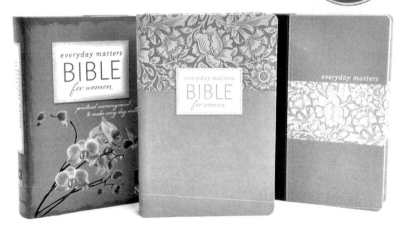

Over 300 articles interspersed throughout the Scriptures offer wisdom and encouragement as you read.
Hundreds of authors include:

Kay Warren   *Liz Curtis Higgs*   *Joni Eareckson Tada*

Ann Voskamp   *Tim Keller*   *Priscilla Shirer*

The perfect companion to the
Everyday Matters Bible Studies for Women

HENDRICKSON
PUBLISHERS